World Book, Inc.
233 N. Michigan Avenue
Chicago, IL 60601
U.S.A.

For information about other World Book publications, visit our Web site at **http://www.worldbookonline.com** or call **1-800-WORLDBK (967-5325)**.
For information about sales to schools and libraries, call **1-800-975-3250 (United States),** or **1-800-837-5365 (Canada)**.

Editorial:
Editor in Chief: Paul A. Kobasa
Project Managers: Cassie Mayer, Michael Noren
Editor: Jake Bumgardner
Content Development: Odyssey Books
Writer: Rebecca McEwen
Researcher: Cheryl Graham
Manager, Contracts & Compliance
  (Rights & Permissions): Loranne K. Shields
Indexer: David Pofelski

Graphics and Design:
Associate Director: Sandra M. Dyrlund
Manager, Graphics and Design: Tom Evans
Coordinator, Design Development and Production:
  Brenda B. Tropinski
Designer: Matthew Carrington
Contributing Photographs Editor: Carol Parden
Senior Cartographer: John M. Rejba

Pre-Press and Manufacturing:
Director: Carma Fazio
Manufacturing Manager: Steven K. Hueppchen
Production/Technology Manager: Anne Fritzinger

Picture Acknowledgment:
Front Cover: NASA/ESA/STScI/J. Hester and P. Scowen, Arizona State University
Back Cover: Art Resource

AKG Images 22; © B.A.E. Inc/Alamy Images 12; © mediacolor's/Alamy Images 35; © Skyscan Photolibrary/Alamy Images 9; © Stock Connection Blue/Alamy Images 36; © vario images GmbH/Alamy Images 37; (c) AP/Wide World 23; Art Resource 4, 20; © DeA Picture Library/Art Resource, 8; Bridgeman Art Library 13, 21; © AFP/Getty Images 33, 43; © National Geographic/Getty Images 15; Granger Collection 7, 13, 14, 17, 18, 25, 27, 31; © Roger-Viollet, Image Works 28; (c) Lomonosov Museum 22; NASA 12, 16, 32, 38, 39, 40; Jeff Hester and Paul Scowen, Arizona State University/NASA 41; NASA and The Hubble Heritage Team (AURA/STScI) 28, 40; NASA/GSFC 29; NASA/JPL 27; National Optical Astronomy Observatory 7; National Park Service 11; Oregon Scientific, Inc. 37; © John Chumack, Photo Researchers 5; © Detlev Van Ravenswaay, Photo Researchers 43; © Mark Garlick, Photo Researchers 26; (c) David A. Hardy, Futures: 50 Years in Space/SPL/Photo Researchers 31; © David Parker, Photo Researchers 5; Shutterstock 10, 24, 44; Turtle Bay Exploration Park, Redding, CA 11;

All maps and illustrations are the exclusive property of World Book, Inc.

Library of Congress Cataloging-in-Publication Data
Astronomy.
    p. cm. –   (Inventions and discoveries)
  Includes index.
  Summary: "An exploration of the transformative impact of inventions and discoveries in the field of astronomy. Features include fact boxes, sidebars, biographies, timeline, glossary, list of recommended reading and Web sites, and index"–Provided by publisher.
  ISBN 978-0-7166-0387-0
  1. Astronomy–Juvenile literature. 2. Astronomy–History–Juvenile literature.
I. World Book, Inc.
QB46.A879 2009
520–dc22
                            2008040649

Inventions and Discoveries
Set ISBN: 978-0-7166-0380-1
Printed in China
1 2 3 4 5 12 11 10 09

▶ Table of Contents

There is a glossary of terms on pages 45-46. Terms defined in the glossary are in type **that looks like this** on their first appearance on any spread (two facing pages).

Introduction

What is an invention?

An invention is a new device, new product, or new way of doing something. Inventions change the way people live. Before the car was invented, travel by horseback was common. Before the light bulb was invented, people used candles and similar sources of light to see at night. Almost two million years ago, the creation of the spear and the bow and arrow helped people hunt better. Later, the invention of new farming methods allowed people to stay in one place instead of wandering around in search of food. People then created villages and invented ways to travel to other villages, making trade possible. Today, inventions continue to change the way we live.

What is astronomy?

From the earliest times, people have searched the sky for explanations, for clues to our own existence, and for answers to the mysteries of our natural world. Long before **telescopes,** space exploration, and the advances of modern science, ancient people told stories of the sun, the moon, and the stars. They learned the moon's cycles and examined the positions of the stars. Early astronomers saw patterns in groups of stars that looked like familiar animals, people, or things. The stories they told to explain these shapes became their **mythology.**

Early astronomers invented many tools to help them study objects in the sky.

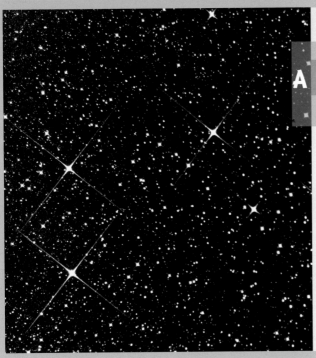

Other stars and galaxies are so many billions of miles away from Earth that astronomers measure the distances in **light-years.** One light-year is how far light can travel during the length of year. That is pretty far, considering light travels at 186,282 miles (299,792 kilometers) per second! If a star is four light-years away, the light we see is four years old. When we gaze upon a star 2 million light-years away, we are looking at light that is 2 million years old. Looking at the stars is like looking back in time!

Powerful telescopes, like this one (right) at the Leuschner Observatory in California, let us gaze into the universe.

These early observations became the basis for the science of astronomy—the study of the **universe** beyond Earth, and the objects out there in it.

Modern astronomers use powerful telescopes to learn how far away other stars and **galaxies** are. They study planets and **comets** (bright objects with starlike centers) to discover how they move through the **solar system.** They study new and ancient galaxies and guess at how the universe began, looking ever deeper into the universe, and looking back in time itself.

▶ Constellations

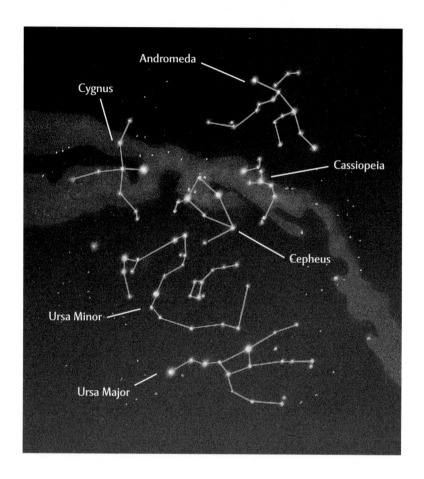

Andromeda

Cygnus

Cassiopeia

Cepheus

Ursa Minor

Ursa Major

Constellations help people identify the stars, and they fill the sky with mythical personalities.

Ancient people spent a lot of time looking up at the night sky. Eventually they noticed that many stars stuck together in groups, or **constellations.** A constellation is a collection of stars that, dot-to-dot, make a visible pattern. People saw how many of these stars and constellations appeared at different times of the year and at different places in the night sky. Some stars and constellations became associated with the time of year when crops were planted or harvested (cut and gathered). Others appeared only in winter or summer, or, in Egypt, when the Nile flooded each year.

In ancient Greece, stargazers created a whole system of constellations and myths. Most of the constellations seen in the **Northern Hemisphere** were first identified by the Greeks. The **Southern Hemisphere** cannot be seen from Greece, so the constellations there were named by different people—many of them European explorers sailing the south seas for the first time.

The names of constellations come from their shapes as well as the times of year they appear. Capricorn (the water goat), Aquarius (the water bearer), and Pisces (fishes) make up the "wet quarter" of the year—the modern months of January, February, and March, when many places get the most rain or snow. If you connect the dots of stars, you'll see that they look like their names.

Ptolemy

Ptolemy (A.D. 100?-165?) was an astronomer in Alexandria, Egypt. Ptolemy wrote the *Almagest*, the oldest surviving book on astronomy. It contains accurate charts and catalogs of planets and stars, as well as a list of 48 constellations. However, his model of the **universe** was geocentric, meaning that Earth was at its center. Ptolemy's model was believed to be accurate until the 1500's, when a Polish astronomer named Nicolaus Copernicus developed the theory that Earth revolved around the sun.

People all over the world came up with their own constellations and systems of **astrology.** The Incas and the Australian Aborigines, for example, formed constellations out of dark **nebulae** (space clouds made of dust and gas), as well as stars. The "Emu in the Sky" is a dark cloud that stretches through the stars of the Southern Cross constellation.

A nebula is usually the beginning—or end—of a star.

► Calendar Stones

Many ancient **civilizations** created calendars based on the stars, the sun, and the moon. The Maya, ancient Egyptians, and ancient **Romans** are famous for their calendars. However, the Salisbury Plain in England is home to perhaps the most famous calendar of them all: Stonehenge.

Around 3100 B.C., the site of Stonehenge began as a ceremonial ditch within a low, circular wall of earth. Fifty-six holes ran along the inner edge of the enclosure. By moving a wooden post twice a day, ancient people could track the 28-day cycle of the moon. The holes could also be used to predict both **lunar** and **solar eclipses.** Around 2600 B.C., people added a small circle of volcanic rocks called bluestones to the center of the site. Later builders

This drawing recreates the difficult construction of Stonehenge.

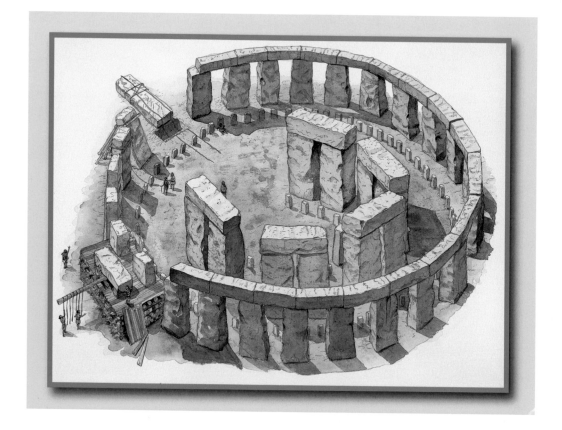

constructed an outer circle of huge gray sandstones called sarsens. A gap through all the circles opens in the exact spot of the midsummer sunrise and the midwinter sunset. Though Stonehenge was used as a gathering place and religious center, it also worked as an astronomical calendar, and perhaps as an **observatory,** as well.

The people who built Stonehenge started simply enough, digging the trench (ditch) with animal bones, stones, and wooden tools. But carrying the stones was a huge challenge. The inner circle of bluestones probably came from mountains in Wales some 245 miles (395 kilometers) away, and the giant sarsen stones came from about 20 (32 kilometers) miles away. Without the benefit of the wheel, getting these stones to the site and then lifting them into position was an enormously difficult task.

Since there is no writing from this period, no one knows for sure why Stonehenge was built, or even who built it. But the sheer difficulty of the project shows that it was of great importance. Several other stone circles, or henges, were built across England, but Stonehenge is by far the largest and most awe-inspiring.

The Maya, American Indian people who lived in Central America and south Mexico, had three different calendars. One was a 365-day solar calendar, much like the calendar we use today. It accounted for everyday things like rainy and dry seasons and planting and harvesting crops. Another calendar was a sort of sacred book, with 260 days, that was used to predict the moods of the gods. The third calendar was known as the "long count." It was a continuous record of history beginning with August 11, 3114 B.C. This date is about the same time that Stonehenge was built. In fact, several great civilizations marked this period as their beginning.

The ruins of Stonehenge remain a popular tourist attraction.

▶ Sundials

Though calendars could tell you the time of year, a more exact device was needed to tell the time within a day. The rising and setting of the sun served as a general indicator, but as **civilization** developed, people needed more specific information about the time.

About 4,000 years ago, people in ancient Babylon in present-day Iraq developed **sundials.** These early timepieces were very simple. A sundial had a dial face, divided into 12 parts, and a flat pointer that stuck up in the air. During the day, the sun shone against the pointer, which cast a shadow. As the sun moved across the sky from east to west, the pointer's shadow moved from one side of the dial to the other, crossing each of the twelve sections. The shadow pointed into the first section of the dial face at sunrise, and into the twelfth section at sunset. This meant there were twelve blocks of time, or "hours," during each day.

The early sundials had problems, however. Summer days are much longer than winter days, and the amount of sun also varies by where you are on Earth. On the **equator,** the amount of daylight changes very little. But nearer the North and South Poles, daylight is greatly reduced in winter and extended in summer. These variations are caused by Earth's curvature (roundness), its tilt on its **axis,** and its continual move-

Sundials were the earliest form of keeping time within a day.

About 1,000 years ago, in what is now the southwestern United States, the Pueblo Indian peoples of New Mexico developed a unique sundial known as the "Sun Dagger." The Pueblo Indians made the Sun Dagger on a rock on top of the Fajada Butte in the Chaco Canyon. The rock was marked with a spiral carving. Three vertical (upright) slabs of rock in front of the sundial caused a dagger of light to appear at certain points on the spiral, depending on the time of year. The Pueblo Indians used the Sun Dagger to keep track of the changing seasons and to help them plan when to plant crops. They also used it to keep track of when certain seasonal ceremonies should be held.

ment around the sun. To deal with these issues, later sundials had pointers that slanted at an angle to match the **latitude** of the location, and the time was read in "temporary hours" that changed with the seasons.

When people invented mechanical clocks in the A.D. 1300's, they learned how to make sundials that measured hours of an equal length—"equal hours"—no matter what the time of year. These sundials were so exact that people often used them to reset their mechanical clocks.

The Sundial Bridge is a modern-day sundial. It crosses the Sacramento River in California.

▶ Earth Is Round

In ancient times, people believed that Earth was flat. Some believed it was a sort of giant disc floating in the ocean. But in the 300's B.C., the Greek philosopher Aristotle suspected otherwise. While watching a **lunar eclipse,** he saw that Earth's shadow on the moon was shaped like a circle. He reasoned, then, that Earth must be a giant sphere (ball).

Additional proof followed. Sailors noticed that they could see only the top of a ship on the **horizon,** meaning that the sea must curve along the surface of a spherical Earth. People

Astronomers first discovered that Earth was round more than 2,000 years ago.

Because Earth is round, people in the Northern and Southern Hemispheres see different stars in the night sky.

also found that the length of an object's shadow grew longer the farther away it was from the **equator.** Also, different **constellations** were seen on each side of the equator.

Though most scientists after Aristotle agreed that Earth was round, some people refused to accept it. To the ancient **Roman** poet and philosopher Lucretius (*loo KREE shih uhs*), it seemed ridiculous to imagine that one side of the planet enjoyed bright daylight while the other side was in darkness. He argued that the oceans would spill right off of Earth if it were round instead of flat.

The idea of a round Earth made possible the Age of Discovery, a period of great European exploration that began in the 1400's. During this

period, Christopher Columbus crossed the Atlantic Ocean, and Ferdinand Magellan circled the entire globe.

In 1969, the American astronauts Neil Armstrong and Buzz Aldrin landed on the moon. From there, they took photographs of Earth that showed our planet as it appears from space: beautifully blue and round like a marble.

ERATOSTHENES
En Dactylioth Lippert.

Eratosthenes

Eratosthenes (276?-195? B.C.) was a Greek mathematician who figured out how to measure the circumference of (distance around) Earth. Using his understanding of mathematics and the measurements of shadows, he guessed that Earth was 24,235 miles (39,002 kilometers) around. His guess was quite accurate. Today, we know that Earth is 24,901.55 miles (40,075.16 kilometers) around at the equator. Eratosthenes also created the system of **latitude** and **longitude.**

▶ The Stars as Guides

After thousands of years of studying the stars, people became familiar with their movements and patterns. For example, Polaris—also known as the North Star, or Pole Star—never seemed to move in the sky, even though all the other stars seemed to shift positions. Eventually, people knew that when they faced Polaris, they were facing north.

This kind of knowledge became very helpful as people started mapping the lands they encountered during their journeys. By looking into the sky, travelers could get a general idea of what direction they were heading. However, as people began to explore further into the oceans, they needed more exact measurements.

Around 130 B.C., astronomers started using an instrument called an **astrolabe** to measure exactly how high stars sat above the **horizon** each

This 1575 wood-cut shows sailors using the stars to navigate the seas.

An astrolabe has a map of the stars on its surface to match with the night sky.

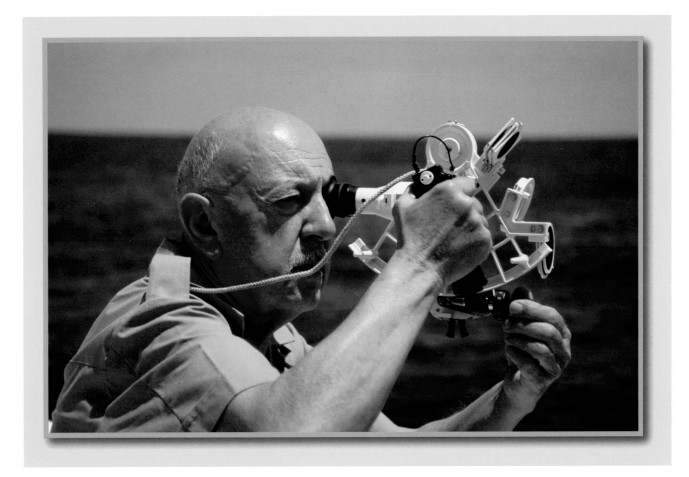

night. This tool became very useful to ocean travelers, who used it to measure stars' positions, check these positions against their charts, and then figure out their **latitude.** For the next 1,800 years, navigators used astrolabes to guide their ships on journeys around the world.

About 1757, John Campbell of the British Royal Navy invented a device called the **sextant,** which was based upon the work of earlier inventors. A sextant uses angles to measure the distance between two points, such as between the sun and the horizon. It could be used to find a location's latitude, and, with the aid of an accurate clock, its **longitude** as well.

Celestial navigation is the method of finding direction and position by measuring the angles between the horizon and objects in the sky, like the moon or stars. The **coordinates** of these heavenly bodies are listed in books called almanacs.

The sextant was the most important navigation tool until the mid-1900's. Today, navigators can use many different **electronic** tools that use **radio signals** to find their way.

Sextants measure the distance and angle of stars from the horizon.

The Modern Calendar

For ages, people have kept track of months and years according to the regular cycles of the moon. A **lunar month** is the period from one full moon to the next, and it lasts about 29.5 days. Twelve lunar months amount to 354 days. However, this number is about 11 days shorter than a true **solar year,** which lasts 365 days, 5 hours, 48 minutes, and 46 seconds. This difference caused great confusion. A calendar based on 12 lunar months quickly fell out of line with the seasons. Some people attempted to correct the problem by making some years 12 months long and other years 13 months long.

In 46 B.C., the ancient **Roman** leader Julius Caesar introduced the Julian calendar. The old calendar had gotten so off track that the "winter" lunar months were starting in what we now know as September, and the "autumn" months began when the summer days were at their longest. Caesar worked with astronomers to solve this

The phases of the moon indicate the moon's location in relation to Earth and the sun. People used the phases of the moon to create early calendars.

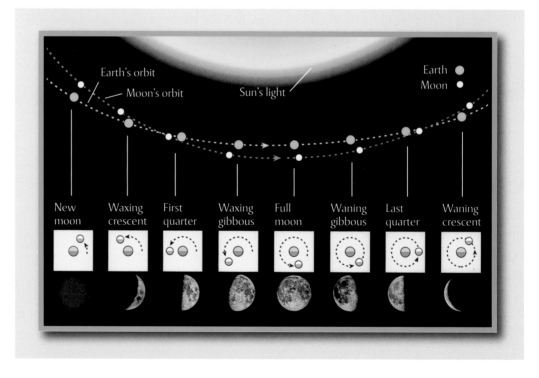

problem. They came up with a new calendar that had 12 months of 31 and 30 days, except for February, which had 29 days. Every fourth year, February would get 30 days—the first **leap year.** Meanwhile, the "year" 46 B.C. had 445 days so that the next year would align properly with the new calendar. Later, one day was removed from February and added to August.

People used the Julian calendar for more than 1,600 years. It was nearly accurate, but not perfect. Each Julian year lasted exactly 365 days—which is about 11 minutes and 14 seconds longer than a true solar year. After 1,600 years of using the Julian calendar, these minutes had added up and the calendar was 10 days off again.

In 1582, Pope Gregory XIII corrected this difference by cutting 10 days out of that year's month of October, jumping right from October 4 to October 15. Then, to make sure that this type of correction would not have to happen again, he decided that the month of February would get one extra day in any century year that can be divided by 400. For example, in 1600 and 2000, February got an extra day. This **Gregorian calendar** is so accurate that it only differs from the solar year by 0.53 seconds every 100 years.

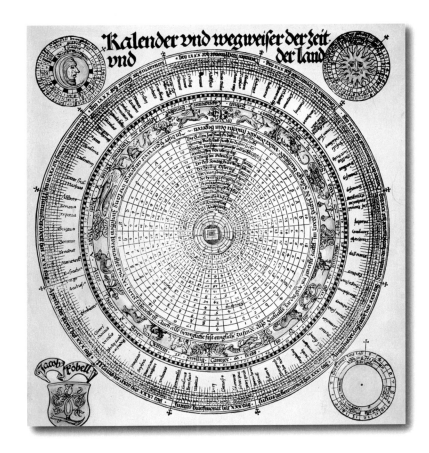

Other calendars in use today include the Chinese, Islamic, and Hebrew calendars. Many other cultures keep calendars to mark religious and cultural events.

The Julian Calendar is depicted in this German print from 1520.

F U N   F A C T
The month of July is named after Julius Caesar. The month of August is named after Augustus, Rome's first emperor. According to tradition, Augustus adjusted the Julian calendar so that his month, August, would have the same number of days as Caesar's month, July. The additional day for August was taken from February, so that February had 28 days.

▶ The Telescope

The Italian astronomer Galileo made many important observations through his telescope, including the discovery that Saturn has rings.

A Dutch **optician** named Hans Lippershey probably built the first **telescope** in 1608. He put two glass lenses in a narrow tube and, looking through it, found that it doubled the distance he could see with only one lens. This was the first **refracting telescope**—a kind of telescope that refracts, or bends, light by passing it through a thick glass lens.

Less than a year later, the Italian astronomer Galileo (*GAL uh LAY oh*) built a telescope with three lenses and turned it to the sky. Impressed by what he saw, he searched for ways to make his telescope even better. Galileo soon demonstrated a telescope that was eight times as powerful as the human eye.

By autumn of 1609, Galileo was studying the skies with telescopes that magnified objects by 20 times. He was the first to see that the surface of the moon was rough and had craters (holes in the ground). Galileo discovered the four largest moons orbiting Jupiter, as well as the rings around Saturn.

Telescope technology improved rapidly. By 1668, the English scientist Sir Isaac Newton had built a **reflecting telescope.** This type of telescope uses mirrors instead of lenses. The magnified image is sharper in a reflecting telescope, because it does not need to pass through a series of thick glass lenses. Light from a star simply reflects off a bowl-shaped mirror to form an enlarged image within the telescope. This light is then seen through the eyepiece, which magnifies it further.

The telescopes of Galileo and Newton were **optical telescopes.** In other words, they read and interpret

Galileo Galilei

Galileo Galilei (1564–1642), an Italian astronomer, studied much more than the stars. He was an expert mathematician and a philosopher. He believed that anything that occurred in nature could be measured mathematically. Because of his work, scientists since his time have used experimentation to prove the facts of nature.

Galileo's observations of the night sky led him to believe that Earth may not be the center of the **universe**—knowledge that went against the teachings of the Catholic Church at that time. In 1633, Galileo was condemned to life imprisonment by a special court that tried people who were believed to be against the Catholic Church. Though Galileo never ended up in an actual prison, he did spend the rest of his life under house arrest outside of Florence, Italy.

light, much like the human eye does. Today's modern telescopes are built to "see" things that our eyes cannot, such as **radio waves** and **X rays.** Many objects, like some **quasars** and other sources of energy, give off these kinds of rays rather than visible light. With **radio telescopes,** we can hear them, sense them, and record them just as if we could see them.

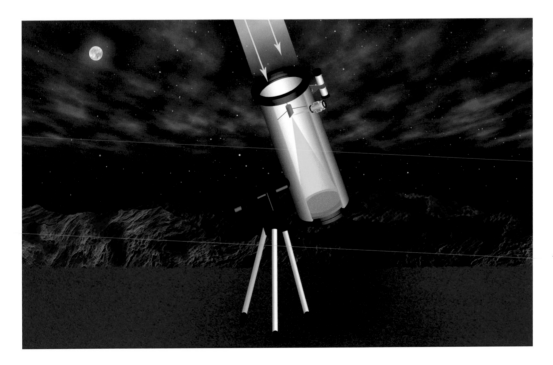

Optical telescopes contain a mirror or lens that collects light and uses it to form an image.

The Solar System

From left to right: Mercury, Venus, Earth, Mars, Jupiter, Saturn, Uranus, Neptune.

The eight planets of our solar system are kept in line by the massive sun.

In the early 1600's, the Catholic Church still insisted that Earth was the center of the **universe,** and that everything else revolved around it. Astronomers, however, had built a strong case against this idea.

Tycho Brahe (right) and Johannes Kepler (left) explained the solar system.

Nicolaus Copernicus, in the early 1500's, was the first to suggest that Earth and other planets revolved around the sun. But because these ideas did not fit in with the universe described by the Bible, the church punished people who tried to prove them. Galileo, who supported Copernicus's theories, was arrested by the church and forced to say that such ideas were untrue.

In the late 1500's and early 1600's, Johannes (*yoh HAHN uhs*) Kepler, a German astronomer and mathematician, was doing much the same work as Galileo. Kepler, how-

Nicolaus Copernicus

Nicolaus Copernicus (1473–1543) was a Polish astronomer who first proposed that Earth is a planet, and that planets orbit around a star, such as the sun. He also guessed, rightly, that Earth turns once each day on its own **axis.**

Copernicus came from a wealthy merchant family, and he was trained for a career as a church official. While he studied, he developed a passion for astronomy. His viewpoints conflicted with the church's ideas on the universe, but they created a basis on which every later astronomer would build.

ever, was careful to back up his scientific conclusions with religious arguments. As a result, he met with less resistance from the church.

Kepler worked with the Danish astronomer Tycho (*TEE koh*) Brahe, who had spent years studying the movement of Mars. Kepler eventually figured out the basic way that such planets as Mars could travel around a "parent" star, such as the sun.

Kepler became convinced that Copernicus's theories on planetary movement must be true. Though it was a dangerous thing to do at the time, Kepler publicly announced that Earth and other planets travel around the sun. He even published a textbook on the subject in 1621.

Kepler's studies led to the birth of modern astronomy. Today, it is accepted that the sun is the center of the **solar system,** and that Earth and seven other planets travel in an oval-shaped orbit around it.

Kepler's Laws of Planetary Motion

Every planet follows an oval-shaped orbit around the sun. This path is called an ellipse.

Planets move faster when they are closer to the sun, and slower when they are farther away from the sun.

The time it takes a planet to orbit the sun once is called a period. The length of the period can help astronomers figure out the planet's distance from the sun.

▶ Planetariums

The Gottorp Globe contained a map of Earth on the outside and a map of the universe on the inside.

A **planetarium** is a building or room that houses a model of the **universe.** *Planetarium* also refers to a device that projects representations of planets and other objects in the universe. Early planetariums were either mechanical models that represented the stars and planets or movable pictures of the starry sky that were painted on the inside of domed roofs.

One of the first planetariums was the Gottorp Globe, built in Germany in the mid-1600's. The structure was a hollow copper sphere more than 10 feet (3 meters) across, with a curved bench inside. **Constellations** appeared on the inner surface of the sphere, with gold-painted nails representing the stars. **Engineers** figured out how to make the globe rotate, so people inside could watch a model of the night sky pass overhead. Outside, people could see a fairly accurate representation of Earth's rotation.

The Mark I planetarium projector first displayed the universe in 1925 in Munich, Germany.

In the late 1600's, European clockmakers began making small model planetariums. A person could wind up the model and then watch the miniature planets move around the sun.

The invention of electric lights and motors in the late 1800's made it possible to build large model planetariums. One such model was installed at the Deutsches (*DOY chuhs*) Museum in Munich, Germany, in the 1920's. The planetarium included a model sun at the center of a circular room. Model planets were suspended from the room's ceiling by rods and moved around the sun with motorized cars.

In 1925, the first modern planetarium **projector** was installed at the Deutsches Museum. The device, called the Mark I, included a rotating hollow metal sphere known as a star ball, which used 31 lenses to display stars on the dome. Attached to the star ball were seven additional projectors, which displayed images of the planets, the sun, and the moon.

Today, modern planetariums show the universe by using lifelike images from **digital** projectors. These projectors can show what the universe looks like both from Earth and from other places in the universe.

The most advanced planetarium projectors can create images as sharp and as precise in color as the actual stars as seen from a high mountain. One such device, a Zeiss Mark IX at the Hayden Planetarium in the Rose Center for Earth and Space in New York City, can project images of more than 9,000 stars. The projector has 32 star plates. Light for each star travels from a central lamp through an optical fiber, a hair-thin strand of glass. Because the fiber is so tiny, the image on the dome is pointlike—just like a real star in the sky. Separate projectors steered by computer-controlled motors create images of the sun, the moon, and the planets.

The Rose Center for Earth and Space features the spectacular Hayden Planetarium.

► The Law of Gravitation

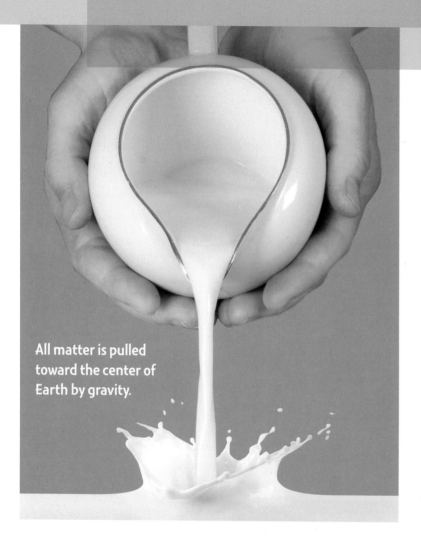

All matter is pulled toward the center of Earth by gravity.

What exactly is it that links the planets to the sun? And why do moons orbit the planets? For years, some people guessed that the sun and the planets possessed a sort of strong **magnetic force** that drew them all together. Others suggested that a giant **celestial** whirlpool kept everything spinning in a certain order.

In 1665, a brilliant young English scientist named Isaac Newton watched an apple fall. He began to wonder what caused the apple to come down from the tree. Newton guessed that there must be some sort of force behind it, something natural that pulls things toward the ground. This turned out to be **gravitation,** or the force of gravity. Gravitation is the natural force that pulls objects toward the planet's center.

Gravitation depends on an object's **mass,** which is often defined as the amount of matter in an object. An elephant has much greater mass than a mouse, just like the gigantic planet Jupiter has greater mass than a smaller planet like Mercury. Objects

Sir Isaac Newton

Sir Isaac Newton (1642–1727) was a famous English scientist, astronomer, and mathematician. Newton completely changed people's understanding of how the **universe** works. He unlocked the secret to what holds the universe together through his theory of gravitation. He also discovered the secrets of light and color, and was one of the people who invented an entirely new kind of math called calculus.

Despite his many accomplishments, Newton remained modest throughout his life. Shortly before his death, Newton said, "I do not know what I may appear to the world, but to myself I seem to have been only like a boy playing on the seashore, and diverting myself in now and then finding a smoother pebble or a prettier shell than ordinary, whilst the great ocean of truth lay all undiscovered before me."

with larger masses have greater forces of gravity. The sun, which has a mass many times larger than Earth's, has a gravitational pull strong enough to hold everything in the **solar system** in orbit around it.

Gravity also depends on the distance between two objects. Gravity on the surface of Earth is much stronger than it is hundreds of miles out in space. Similarly, the sun's gravitational pull on Earth is stronger than it is on Saturn, which is much farther away.

Newton's law of gravitation set forth the relationship between gravity, mass, and distance. His work answered a lot of questions that people had never before been able to understand. It explained why water stays in the oceans, why the sun's hot gases don't escape into space, and why people and things don't fly off Earth's surface.

Gravity is strongest at the center of a planet and lessens over distance.

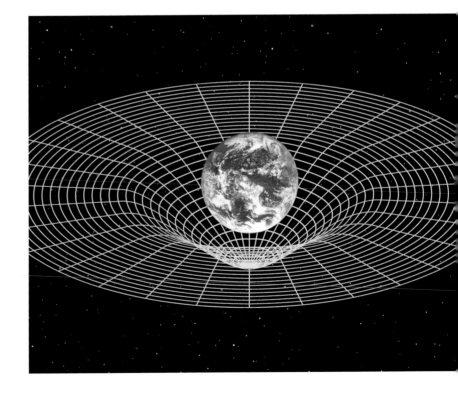

The Seventh Planet: Uranus

Uranus is the farthest planet from the sun that can be seen without a telescope.

comets are close enough to Earth that they get bigger when viewed through strong telescopes.

To Herschel's surprise, his mysterious "star" did indeed look larger when viewed through the more powerful telescope. He thought he had discovered a comet. He watched it for a month, noting that the object looked larger each night. He measured how far it traveled across the sky each night, and he learned how to predict its path.

At that time, the known **solar system** was made up of the sun, Earth, and five other planets: Mercury, Venus, Mars, Jupiter, and Saturn. When Herschel presented his findings to a scientific organization of London, they soon realized that his "comet" was actually a seventh planet. It was named Uranus, after the Greek god of the sky.

Uranus is a giant ball of gas and liquid, about 14 times the size of Earth. It has numerous moons and is circled by a system of rings. Uranus spins much faster than Earth, com-

In March of 1781, the British astronomer William Herschel was studying a small cluster of stars. He noticed that one of the stars seemed much larger than the others around it. He then changed to a stronger **telescope.** Most stars are so far away that they appear the same size no matter how strong the telescope is. However, planets and

From 1789 to 1845, Herschel's telescope was the biggest, most advanced telescope in the world.

pleting a day (one complete rotation) in only 17 hours. Uranus is the most distant planet that people can see without a telescope. At its closest point, it is 1.7 billion miles (2.7 billion kilometers) from Earth. At its brightest, it looks like a blue-green point of light in the sky.

Uranus is so far from Earth that it is difficult to study. Most of what we know about it comes from images and information sent back by Voyager II, an American spacecraft that flew just 50,000 miles (88,500 kilometers) above the planet's surface in 1986.

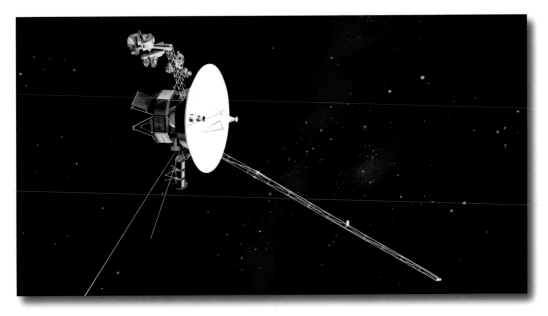

It took just four years for Voyager II to travel from Earth to Saturn, but it took another five years for it to reach Uranus.

▶ The Messier Catalog

This spiral galaxy is Messier Object 100. It is part of the Virgo Cluster, a group of more than 2,000 galaxies.

I n 1784, the French astronomer Charles Messier published the *Catalogue of Nebulae and of Star Clusters.* It listed 110 nonstellar objects, most of which Messier had found on his own. Nonstellar objects include **galaxies, nebulae,** and star clusters. Messier, the chief astronomer of the Marine Observatory in Paris, was working to catalog, or record, all the nonstellar objects visible in the **Northern Hemisphere.**

Messier's original intention was simply to find and record **comets.** But while he was searching for comets, he kept noticing hazy objects that did not seem to change position. These objects were not stars or planets, and they were not comets either. Unsure of what they were, Messier began recording their positions simply so they would not confuse other astronomers.

Messier put down his sightings and discoveries as they occurred. He began with a huge cloud of gas and dust that had come from a **supernova** (exploding star). This cloud is

Charles Messier set out to find comets, but he discovered an entire universe of mysterious objects.

known as the Crab Nebula, or Messier Object One or M1. Some of Messier's more famous entries include the spiral galaxy of Andromeda (M31) and the star cluster of the Pleiades (M45). Because these objects can be studied through a relatively small **telescope,** they have become extremely popular among amateur (nonprofessional) astronomers.

Although Messier is best known for his catalog, he also discovered 13 comets and studied many more. Today, his catalog remains an important source for professional and amateur astronomers alike. Some astronomers participate in Messier "marathons," where they try to find as many of the 110 Messier objects as they can in one night.

The *New General Catalogue* (NGC) was published in 1888 as an update and extension of Messier's catalog. The British astronomer William Herschel and his son John added most of the NGC's 8,000 objects. Two later *Index Catalogues* added 5,000 more. The list continues to grow as new technologies allow us to reach, see, and listen deeper into space.

The Crab Nebula was Messier's first recorded object. The above image was taken by the Hubble Space Telescope in 2008.

▶ The Eighth Planet: Neptune

Astronomers at first mistook Neptune's blue, swirling surface for water.

Neptune, the eighth planet, is the farthest planet from the sun. It is bright blue and circled by rings. Like Uranus, it is an "ice giant," made mostly of frozen liquids and gases. Neptune has a mysterious "Great Dark Spot" that appears to be a hole in the planet's **atmosphere.** The cold winds around this spot are estimated to blow at 1,500 miles (2,400 kilometers) per hour. With low temperatures, violent storms, and racing clouds, Neptune is a very cold and dark place.

Galileo made a drawing of Neptune in 1612, but he thought it was a star. It would be another 200 years before two astronomers discovered that it was a planet. John C. Adams in England and Urbain J. J. Leverrier in France were studying Uranus, when they noticed a strange bump in that planet's orbit. They guessed that the bump was caused by the **gravitational** pull of an eighth planet. Using complex mathematics, they each guessed where this planet should be. In 1846, astronomers followed their directions and found Neptune.

Leverrier named the planet Neptune after the **Roman** god of the sea. From Earth, 2.7 billion miles (4.3 billion kilometers) away, Neptune's bright, swirling clouds look like water. In fact, scientists believe Neptune may indeed have water on it—though the water would be frozen, to be sure.

The average temperature on Neptune is around -328 °F (-200 °C). It would be even colder, but scientists believe Neptune has a heated core (center), just like Earth does. It is 17 times the size of Earth, and it takes nearly 165 Earth years for it to circle the sun.

The discovery of Neptune was interesting, because it was based purely on reasoning, mathematics, and the science of astronomy. The planet was not seen first and then explained. Instead, astronomers reasoned that *it must be there*—and then they found it.

With the help of mathematics, Urbain Leverrier (right) helped pinpoint the location of Neptune.

A CLOSER LOOK

Neptune has at least 13 moons. Triton, the largest, is the only moon in the **solar system** that orbits its planet in the opposite direction of the planet's own orbit. Triton is believed to be the coldest place in the solar system, with an average temperature of -390 °F (-235 °C). It appears to have active volcanoes that shoot out ice crystals instead of lava. Triton won't be around forever, though. Neptune's massive gravitational pull is moving the moon steadily closer and will continue to do so until it tears the moon apart.

The volcanoes of Triton

▶ Black Holes

In this illustration, light and dust are condensed through a black hole into an intense beam.

In 1916, the German-born scientist Albert Einstein published a paper describing something called a **black hole** in the **universe.** The idea was based on his studies of space and time, and it was without any physical proof. But Einstein's studies told him that black holes must exist.

A black hole is a region of space that has a **gravitational** force so strong that nothing can escape from it—not even light. This makes the region lightless, or black. The gravitational force is strong near a black hole because all the black hole's matter is concentrated at a single point in its center. No astronomer has ever seen a black hole. In fact, the term's very definition makes seeing one impossible.

Every planet, moon, and star has gravity. In order for something to escape gravity, it must reach a certain speed. For instance, to escape Earth's gravity, a rocket must travel about 25,000 miles (40,200 kilometers) per hour. The speed necessary to escape a black hole's gravity is greater than the speed of light. And since nothing is faster than light, nothing can escape.

Scientists believe that a black hole is formed when a very large star collapses in on itself. When the star shrinks to a certain point, it explodes and then shrinks more and more. Eventually, all the remaining matter from the star is squeezed into a single point smaller than an **atom.** Imagine our own gigantic sun pressed into something so small that it cannot be seen!

Although a black hole cannot be seen, it is possible to see how it might affect its surroundings. For example, a black hole might pull gas away from a nearby star, causing the star to heat up. The heat then gives off **X rays,** which scientists can detect with special **telescopes.**

No one has yet discovered a black hole for certain, but scientists have come across mysterious spots in space that might be black holes. Scientists guess that the Milky Way **galaxy,** home to our own **solar system,** may contain millions of black holes.

The Milky Way is thought to center around a huge black hole that

keeps the galaxy together and spinning, just as the sun does in our solar system. Scientists believe that most other galaxies also have a huge black hole at the center.

Albert Einstein

Albert Einstein (1879-1955) was one of the greatest scientists in human history. Einstein developed entirely new ideas on matter, energy, space, and time. In a way, Einstein worked backwards. Most scientists begin with a problem, study it, and use mathematics to solve or explain the problem. Einstein would begin with a complex mathematical idea and then predict how it might be used in the universe. This is how he came up with such an original idea as the black hole. Without having thought of the idea of a black hole, how would anyone ever suspect they were there?

▶ Time Zones

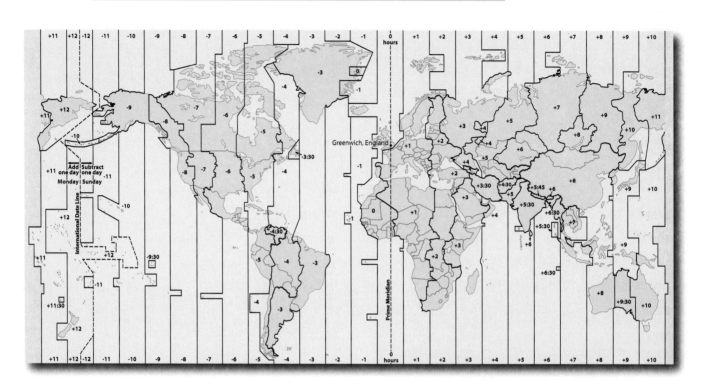

Earth is divided into 24 time zones—one for each hour of the day.

As transportation and communication improved throughout history, it became important for people to keep common time with others who were far away. But because only one side of Earth can face the sun at any given time, it cannot be daylight everywhere at once. As a result, people had to develop systems for keeping different times at different locations. Otherwise, some places would experience noon in the middle of the night, or midnight during the day.

In the past, cities and towns set their own time, based on when the sun appeared overhead. However, this practice caused a great deal of confusion, especially as people traveled from one city to another on railroads. Trains from San Francisco, California, and New York City might arrive in Chicago, Illinois, at different hours, even though they got there at the same time.

In 1883, people representing the Canadian and American railroads set up a system called **standard time.**

Standard time divided Canada and the United States into six large sections, or **time zones,** that ran from north to south. The time zone on the east coast was set at one time, and each zone to the west was set one hour earlier. So, if the eastern zone was 9:00 a.m., the zone just to the west of it would be 8:00 a.m., and the zone to the west of that would be 7:00 a.m.

Standard time worked well and, just a year later, went worldwide. The planet was divided into 24 time zones—one for each hour of the day. The international system of time zones starts from the **Greenwich meridian** (often called the prime meridian), the north-south line that runs through Greenwich, England. Every other line of **longitude** is measured out from Greenwich Mean Time (GMT). Moving east of Greenwich, the time becomes one hour later. Moving west of Greenwich, the time becomes one hour earlier.

Today, most areas around the world use standard time, but there are still a few small countries that use their own time zones.

This line, the Greenwich meridian, is the spot from which all time and longitude is measured.

A scientist inspects an atomic clock at the National Institute of Standards in Boulder, Colorado.

In 1955, scientists figured out a new and extremely accurate way of keeping time. They did so by matching the vibrations of **atoms** to the orbits of the planets in our **solar system.** Certain atoms vibrate with the release and intake of energy, and they do it at a remarkably stable rate. The orbit of the planets is also very stable. After figuring out a way to measure them both, scientists combined them to create a system where one second is divided into more than 9 billion smaller, equal parts.

Traditionally, from **sundials** on up to **standard time,** time has been measured according to Earth's rotation. A new year begins with the repetition of a season, and a new day begins with each sunrise. Atomic time still keeps to those rules, but the job of an **atomic clock** is to keep track of all those tiny fractions of seconds.

More than 50 countries with nearly 300 atomic clocks send their time measurements to the International Bureau of Weights and Measures outside of Paris, France. There, scientists take the average of these measurements to set International Atomic Time. International Atomic Time is the standard by which all time is kept on Earth.

Machines at the Paris Observatory measure atomic time against Earth's rotation. Occasionally, "leap seconds" are added or subtracted, just as **leap years** are used to balance the calendar. Atomic time-keeping is so accurate that it will be wrong by less than one second every 50 million years.

The need for atomic clocks and superaccurate time may not be obvious. For catching a bus or a movie on time, ordinary clocks work just fine. But for sending signals over telephone lines, communicating with **artificial satellites,** and navigating ships and airplanes, a much more exact and reliable time system is necessary. To manage signals traveling at or near the speed of light, atomic clocks are needed to keep the signals separate.

Some companies sell alarm clocks that run on atomic time.

Atomic clocks are used in many important fields, including aviation.

The First Human on the Moon

Astronauts must wear specially designed spacesuits to survive the harsh conditions of space.

The moon is the second brightest thing in the sky, after the sun. It is large enough and close enough to Earth that people can easily see it without a **telescope.** Throughout history, people had become familiar with its shape, its cratered surface, and its different

phases. So, once airplanes were invented, it was natural that people would set their sights higher and seek to fly to the moon.

In the 1950's, several countries began their own space programs, but it was the United States and the country then known as the Soviet Union that made a race out of it. The first spacecraft to reach the moon did not carry human beings. In 1959, a Soviet **probe** called Luna 2 landed on the moon. It was followed in 1962 by an American probe called Ranger 4. Both countries sent up many probes throughout the 1960's.

In 1961, U.S. President John F. Kennedy announced a goal of sending an American safely to the moon by the end of the 1960's. But there were a number of problems that needed to be solved before moon travel would be safe enough for humans. One of the main problems came from the fact that there is no air or wind on the moon. In fact, there's no **atmosphere** at all, making sun and shade temperatures hotter

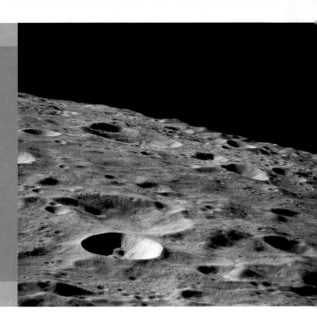
and colder than anything on Earth. Special spacesuits had to be made that would protect an astronaut from harsh temperatures. The suits would also have to provide air to breathe, as well as radio communication.

Finally, in 1969, the American Apollo 11 mission carried the astronauts Neil Armstrong, Michael Collins, and Buzz Aldrin to the moon. On July 20, Armstrong became the first person ever to step onto its surface. His first words have become famous: "That's one small step for a man, one giant leap for mankind." The event captured the attention and imagination of people all over the world.

Between 1969 and 1972, the United States conducted six more Apollo missions, including five landings. The last of those was Apollo 17, in December 1972.

The Saturn V rocket carried each of the moon missions into space.

The Hubble Space Telescope

The Hubble Space Telescope orbits 375 miles (600 kilometers) above the surface of Earth.

The view from Earth into space can be severely limited by **air pollution,** bright city lights, and various conditions in the **atmosphere.** Therefore, the location for an **observatory** needs to be chosen carefully. For years, people looked to build observatories at high altitudes (heights), often in deserts or on mountains away from cities. But eventually, scientists developed a better way for astronomers to look deeper into space.

As scientists at the U.S. National Aeronautics and Space Administration (NASA) improved their ability to send rockets and **artificial satellites** into space, they started to make plans for a special kind of **telescope.** This telescope would not stand on the ground. Instead, it would travel into space and orbit Earth, far above

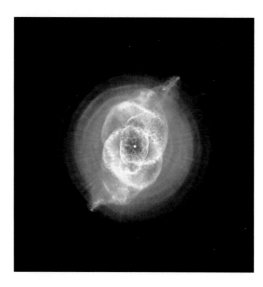

The Cat's Eye Nebula is 3,300 light years from Earth, but through Hubble it looks like it's right next door.

the cloudy atmosphere. Scientists would control the telescope by remote control, so that it could focus in any direction. The telescope would then be able to send back crystal-clear images of distant objects in space.

Eventually, NASA built just such a telescope. In 1990, the **space shuttle** Discovery carried the Hubble Space Telescope into space and launched it into orbit. In 1993, 1997, 1999, and 2002, shuttle astronauts installed extra instruments to the telescope to improve its ability to view and record objects in space.

NASA and the European Space Agency (ESA) together oversee the telescope's operations and maintenance. In addition to sending back amazing photos, the Hubble also has a spectrograph. This device spreads out light into a spectrum (band) of different colors. Scientists back on the ground study this spectrum and measure the amounts of **elements** (like hydrogen and carbon) that are in the light. This helps scientists figure out what distant stars are made of.

The Hubble Space Telescope is named after the American astronomer Edwin P. Hubble. During the 1920's, Hubble's studies greatly increased our understanding of the **universe's** structure and development.

This Hubble photograph of the Eagle Nebula, also called the "Pillars of Creation," shows the slow birth of stars.

A CLOSER LOOK

The National Aeronautics and Space Administration (NASA) is the U.S. government agency that manages the space program. It began in 1958 with the Mercury program, which first put an American astronaut in space. Gemini missions followed, and Apollo took men to the moon and back. The Skylab program showed that people could live and work in a **space station**. The space shuttle program demonstrated a reusable spacecraft that could launch into orbit and land back on Earth like an airplane. Today, NASA continues its work to advance scientific knowledge and develop new technologies.

▶ A Planet Defined

Since Pluto's discovery in 1930, scientists have argued over how to categorize it.

In 2006, a planet disappeared from our **solar system.** There was no major collision, no explosion, nothing shooting into space. The disappearance was caused by astronomers, and the planet that went away was Pluto. Astronomers finally agreed that Pluto was not so much a planet, but merely a large chunk of ice and rock. At best, it is a **dwarf planet**—not a *real* planet, not a moon, but something inbetween.

So, what exactly is a planet? For years, the term had no formal definition in astronomy. But in 2006, the International Astronomical Union

(IAU), a leading organization in astronomy, voted to establish a standard definition. According to this definition, a planet orbits the sun and no other body. It has so much **mass** that its own **gravitational** pull compacts it into a round shape. In addition, a planet has a strong enough gravitational pull to sweep the region of its orbit relatively free of other objects.

Scientists decided that there were crumbs, dwarf planets, and pieces of rock, ice, and dust that were too near and too similar to Pluto. Therefore, Pluto could not be considered a planet.

The argument over Pluto's definition goes back to its discovery in 1930. At that time, many astronomers looked at Pluto's small size and unusual orbit and felt that it was not a normal planet at all. However, other astronomers disagreed. Pluto certainly was a round, planet-shaped body that traveled around the sun. Its gravity seemed to affect the orbits of Neptune and Uranus. And over the years, astronomers found that Pluto had a thin **atmosphere** and was orbited by several small moons. As a result, Pluto was originally declared a planet.

The change in Pluto's status was the result of years of careful study, technological advancement, and steadily growing knowledge.

As scientists observe the skies, they constantly build on information they already have. At times, they encounter something so new and important that it completely changes their beliefs. The skies are full of new discoveries, and there is something special in the stars that makes it hard to look away.

In 2006, members of the International Astronomical Union voted on how to define a planet.

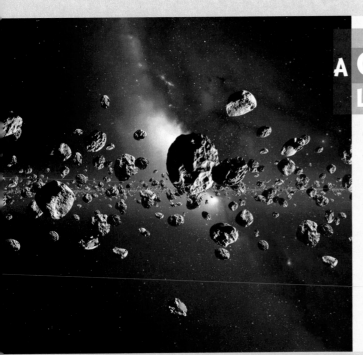

A CLOSER LOOK

Floating in the outer limits of the solar system is a flat ring of icy, small objects that orbit the sun. Called the Kuiper (*KY pur*) belt, it is made up of hundreds of millions of pieces. In fact, this ring is probably made up of whatever was left over when the outer planets formed. Astronomers guess that most **comets** come from this belt. For many years, scientists guessed that there must be just this sort of belt, but they didn't know for sure until the 1990's. Then, **telescopes** captured images that proved it existed. Some of the fragments in the Kuiper belt are tiny flecks of mineral or ice. Other chunks are quite large, measuring more than a hundred miles (161 kilometers) across.

Important Dates in Astronomy

c. 4200 B.C. Egyptian astronomers created the first solar calendar.

c. 3100 B.C. People in England started construction at Stonehenge.

c. 2000 B.C. Sumerian astronomers identified the first constellations.

c. 2000 B.C. The first sundial was created in Babylon.

c. 330 B.C. The Greek philosopher Aristotle used geometry to prove Earth is round.

c. 130 B.C. Astronomers in Greece created the first astrolabe.

46 B.C. The Julian calendar was created.

A.D. 1500's Nicolaus Copernicus of Poland proposes the idea that Earth revolves around the sun.

1582 The Gregorian calendar was created.

Early 1600's Johannes Kepler of Germany described his three laws of planetary motion.

1608 Hans Lippershey of the Netherlands built the first telescope.

Mid-1600's The Gottorp Globe planetarium was constructed in Germany.

1665 Sir Isaac Newton explained the theory of gravitation.

1757 John Campbell of the British Royal Navy invented the sextant.

1781 The British astronomer William Herschel discovered the planet Uranus.

1784 Charles Messier of France published the *Catalogue of Nebulae and of Star Clusters*.

1846 John C. Adams of England and Urbain J. J. Leverrier of France used mathematics to discover the planet Neptune.

1883 Canadian and American railroad representatives created standard time.

1916 The German-born American physicist Albert Einstein explained what black holes are.

1959 The Soviet Union landed a space probe on the moon.

1969 The American astronaut Neil Armstrong became the first human to walk on the moon.

1990 The Hubble Space Telescope was launched into space.

1990's Astronomers saw the Kuiper belt for the first time.

2006 The International Astronomical Union (IAU) created the category of dwarf planets and assigned Pluto to that category.

Glossary

air pollution wastes, resulting largely from the burning of fuel, that dirty the air.

artificial satellite a manufactured object that continuously orbits Earth or some other body in space.

astrolabe an instrument used to measure the angles of celestial bodies above the horizon.

astrology the study of stars and planets to reveal their supposed influence on people or events.

atmosphere the gases that surround a planet or other heavenly body.

atom one of the basic units of matter. An atom is incredibly tiny—more than a million times smaller than the thickness of a human hair.

atomic clock a device for measuring time according to the vibrations of atoms.

axis a straight line about which an object turns. The axis of Earth is an imaginary line through the North Pole and the South Pole.

black hole a region of space that has a gravitational force so strong that nothing can escape from it—not even light.

celestial having to do with the sky.

civilization nations and peoples that have reached advanced stages in social development.

comet a bright object with a starlike center, often with a cloudy tail of light.

constellation a group of stars visible within a particular region of the night sky.

coordinates numbers that define the position of a point.

dwarf planet a round body that orbits a star but does not have enough gravitational pull to be considered a planet.

electronic of or having to do with electrons.

element any substance that contains only one kind of atom.

engineer a person who plans and builds engines, machines, roads, bridges, canals, forts, or the like.

equator the imaginary line that circles Earth halfway between the North and South poles.

galaxy a vast system of stars, gas, dust, and other matter held together in space. The Milky Way is the galaxy that contains Earth, the sun, and other objects in our solar system.

gravitation; gravitational the force of attraction that acts between all objects because of their mass. Because of gravitation, an object that is near Earth falls toward the surface of the planet.

Greenwich meridian also called prime meridian; a north-south line that passes through Greenwich, a part of London, on a map of Earth.

Gregorian calendar the calendar, established by Pope Gregory XIII in 1582, that is used in almost all the world today.

horizon the line where the land and sky seem to meet.

latitude the distance north or south of the equator, measured in degrees.

leap year a year that has 366 days, or one more day than an ordinary year.

light-year a unit used by astronomers to describe distances in space. One light-year equals about 5.88 trillion miles (9.46 trillion kilometers).

longitude the distance east or west on Earth's surface, measured in degrees from a certain line.

lunar eclipse the darkening of the moon that occurs when the moon passes through Earth's shadow.

lunar month the period from one full moon to the next, which equals about 29.5 days.

magnetic force the force that electric currents put on other electric currents. Magnetic force may pull objects together or push them apart.

mass the amount of matter an object has.

mythology a collection of stories, often involving gods, goddesses, and heroes, that attempt to explain natural events.

nebula a cloud of dust particles and gases in space.

Northern Hemisphere all areas of Earth north of the equator.

observatory a research institution where astronomers study planets, stars, galaxies, and other objects in space.

optical telescope a telescope that reads and interprets light, much like the human eye does.

optician a maker or seller of instruments that have to do with the eye or the sense of sight.

phase the shape of the moon or of a planet as it is seen at a particular time.

planetarium a building or room that houses a model of the solar system and universe.

probe a rocket, satellite, or other unmanned spacecraft carrying scientific instruments.

projector a device for projecting an image on a screen.

quasar an extremely bright object at the center of some distant galaxies.

radio signal information that travels through air and space as radio waves.

radio telescope a type of telescope that can detect and record radio waves coming from objects in outer space.

radio wave a pattern of electric and magnetic force that travels through space.

reflecting telescope a type of telescope that uses mirrors instead of lenses.

refracting telescope a kind of telescope that refracts, or bends, light by passing it through a thick glass lens.

Roman of or having to do with ancient Rome or its people. The Roman Empire controlled most of Europe and the Middle East from 27 B.C. to A.D. 476.

sextant an instrument that measures the angular distance between any two points, such as the sun and the horizon.

solar eclipse the apparent darkening of the sun that occurs when the moon passes between the sun and Earth.

solar system a group of heavenly bodies consisting of a star and the planets and other objects orbiting around it.

solar year the time Earth takes to make one complete revolution around the sun.

Southern Hemisphere all areas of Earth south of the equator.

space shuttle a reusable space vehicle for transporting passengers and material.

space station an artificial satellite of Earth designed to be used as an observatory or as a launching site for travel in outer space.

standard time an international system that divides the world into 24 time zones.

sundial one of the oldest known devices for the measurement of time.

supernova an exploding star that can become billions of times as bright as the sun before gradually fading from view.

telescope an instrument for making distant objects appear nearer and larger.

time zone a geographical region within which the same time is used.

universe everything that exists anywhere in space and time.

X rays invisible rays that can be used to produce pictures of bones and other body structures.

► Additional Resources

Books:

- *Amazing Solar System Projects You Can Build Yourself* by Delano Lopez (Nomad Press, 2008).

- *Astronomy* by Kristen Lippincott (DK Eyewitness Books, 2008).

- *How to Enter and Win an Invention Contest* by Edwin J. Sobey (Enslow, 1999).

- *Inventions* by Valerie Wyatt (Kids Can Press, 2003).

- *So You Want to Be an Inventor?* by Judith St. George (Philomel Books, 2002).

- *Sky & Telescope's Pocket Sky Atlas* by Roger W. Sinnott (Sky Publishing, 2006).

Web Sites:

- Amazing Space
  http://amazing-space.stsci.edu
  Learn more about astronomy through activities, explorations, and video on this student Web site. Includes a homework help feature.

- The Best of the Hubble Space Telescope
  http://www.seds.org/hst
  A gallery of some of the best images taken by the Hubble Space Telescope, hosted by the Space Telescope Science Institute.

- Building Planets
  http://www.psi.edu/projects/planets/planets.html
  Theories about the origins of the planets, from the Planetary Science Institute.

- NASA Kids' Club
  http://www.nasa.gov/audience/forkids/kidsclub/flash/index.html
  The U.S. National Aeronautics and Space Administration's (NASA) Web site offers an interactive way for students to explore space.

- National Air and Space Museum
  http://www.nasm.si.edu
  The Smithsonian Institution's National Air and Space Museum Web site includes electronic field trips, activities, and information about current exhibitions.

- National Inventors Hall of Fame
  http://www.invent.org/index.asp
  Information on inventions and inventors from the National Inventors Hall of Fame.

- StarChild
  http://starchild.gsfc.nasa.gov/docs/StarChild/StarChild.html
  A learning center for young astronomers, maintained by the U.S. National Aeronautics and Space Administration.

- Windows to the Universe
  http://www.windows.ucar.edu
  This educational site, presented by the University of Michigan and NASA, covers such topics as planets, stars, and solar systems.

- Women of NASA
  http://quest.arc.nasa.gov/women/intro.html
  This Web site profiles inspirational women who work at NASA in the fields of math, science, and technology.